A History of Logging and Wood Milling in Brazoria County, Texas

A History of Logging and Wood Milling in Brazoria County, Texas

James Smith

A HISTORY OF LOGGING AND WOOD MILLING IN BRAZORIA COUNTY, TEXAS

iUniverse books may be ordered through booksellers or by contacting:

iUniverse
1663 Liberty Drive
Bloomington, IN 47403
www.iuniverse.com
1-800-Authors (1-800-288-4677)

ISBN: 978-1-4917-9956-7 (sc)
ISBN: 978-1-4917-9955-0 (e)

Library of Congress Control Number: 2016911518

Print information available on the last page.

iUniverse rev. date: 12/05/2016

Table of Contents

Dedication

This book is dedicated to the memory of Mr. J.C. Driskill.

(1905-1991)

He was an instructor in the Brazosport Independent School District from 1946-1991.

He taught students the basic life science principles and drivers education. He is, unfortunately, almost forgotten in the Brazosport area, except by the many students that he taught so well.

Preface

This book came to be because the author loves two things, history and trees. The love of history was probably born in him. The love of trees came when his seventh grade biology teacher, Mr. J.C. Driskill, took a seventh grade life science around the Lake Jackson, Texas Junior High School campus. He pointed out the different species of and explained, to some extent what their value was.

By that time, I knew what a saw-mill was. I further grew in forestry knowledge having been in the Boy Scouts of America. In that organization the three lower ranks have some rudimentary requirements about nature and conservation. The upper ranks have several merit badges, some required for Eagle Scout about those subjects. In college I got in on some deeper secrets. In my career as a surveyor, I dealt with trees and forests in other ways.

One day, quite a few years later, I thought "Why doesn't someone write a book about the wood milling industry in this county"? A few years later, it didn't seem this would happen. So I thought "Why not me?" And that's why it is me.

First disclaimer: I'm not what is commonly known as a "tree hugger." However, I do detest wasteful logging practices.

Introduction

Many people in the Brazoria County area, especially newcomers, are unaware that a lumbering industry exists or has ever existed in the county. Books and other types of publications have been written about other industries and enterprises in the county. Examples would be chemicals, sulfur, oil, rice, cattle, and shrimping. Other works mention sawmilling being carried on. For example, James Creighton mentions sawmills in his book A NARRATIVE HISTORY OF BRAZORIA County, Texas The Handbook of Texas, Vol. 1, and several volumes of The TEXAS ALMANAC mention saw mill operations in the county.

This manuscript is the first comprehensive work of wood harvesting and processing in Brazoria County. As much as possible, hard documentation is used. However, this could not always be done. Some of this manuscript, especially pertaining to the earliest times, has had to rely on third hand information and/or incomplete documentation. If the reader can nullify, verify, or otherwise improve on what is stated here, please notify the author. This so that better information can be stated in other editions.

The scope of this manuscript is confined to logging and wood milling, except for the pre-Stephen F. Austin era. Uses of the forests for this time period are mentioned.

Certain related industries such as lumber yards, carpenter-shops, tree services, fire wood and fire-wood cutting are not included and other related businesses are not included in this manuscript.

This manuscript, historically, goes from c. 2500 B.C.E. to 2015. Naturally, there are many huge and unaccountable for time gaps. It is only from the 19th Century and beyond that the picture becomes reasonably clear.

Acknowledgements

The author would like to express his appreciation to several people who made a tough job not quite as tough. First of all, many thanks go to Michael Bailey and Jamie Murray of the Brazoria County historical museum. They gave me a lot of good leads, suggestions, and ideas. Also, thanks to Manuel Stark of Stark Inc. whose firsthand knowledge of his company and the industry proved invaluable. Also, many thanks to Ashley Carter of the Texas historical commission. He helped to fill in many gaps of the plantation era. Sehon Warneke was also highly helpful and co-operative. His knowledge of county things in general gave me lot of good ideas about where to go and whom to ask about what. Nancy Stephens and Nat Hickey gave me valuable information about wood milling in the Freeport area. Many thanks also go to the workers of the Brazoria County Library System, especially the Lake Jackson branch for kind permission to use their facilities. Thanks also go to Mr. Pete Runnels of Churchill for sharing his knowledge of that area. Also helpful were Gerald Shanks of Lake Jackson and Dan Kesnner of Clute for sharing their knowledge of a World War I sawmill near Clute. Pete Alexander of West Columbia and Steve Alexander of Hallettsville shared with me their detailed knowledge of saw milling in and around West Columbia. Thanks, too, to Sandy Rogers with the Texas Prison museum in Huntsville for her co-operation. I'm also grateful to Webb Jones of West Columbia for imparting his knowledge. Also, thanks to the Brazosport College library staff for its helpfulness. Also, the author gives his thanks to the staff of the Brazoria and West Columbia historical museums for their help and co-operation on this project. Very helpful too, was Roy Lewis, professor of English, M.A., Brazosport College for his help with proofreading, grammar, spelling, and punctuation errors.

About the author

James Smith is a 1979 graduate of Sam Houston State University, Huntsville, Tx. He earned a B.S. in Agriculture there in1979. Other qualifications include a few college hours in forestry, loving to run a chain saw, and some experience in the firewood business. Also, he has written a small tree identification manual. It's entitled EASY REFERENCE OF COMMON ORNAMENTAL AND NATIVE TREES IN BRAZORIA COUNTY, TEXAS AND SURROUNDING AREAS. In addition, the author is an Eagle Scout and has three merit badges pertaining to the subject.

Chapter 1

Pre- Columbus To Stephen F. Austin

Forests cover one-fourth to one-third of the surface of Brazoria County. (1) Ever since mankind has set foot in the area, he has made use of the woodlands and its resources.(2)

Karankawan Native Americans are the first ones that European People came across in Texas. Karankawas used the woods primarily as a food source. They gathered pecans and berries. Other uses included various plants for medicines as well as a type of tea made from yaupons. Deer, alligators, and other wild game were hunted. Many other uses were made of the woods too.

For example, cedar was relatively abundant. As shall be seen, it remained so until well into the 20th Century. Cedar was used for making bows. Cane was used for making arrows. It too, was abundant on the Texas Coast for many years. A type of mobile structure was made using a willow pole frame. The poles were 15 to20' long and about 1" thick. Willow wood is very flexible and easy to work. When the frame was built, it was then covered with deer and buffalo hides. It was conceived to be put up and taken down quickly. The Karankawas were a nomadic people and moved about frequently. Other uses of forest resources included the making of dugout canoes from cypress trees. (3)

Later on, explorers and soldiers such as Cabeza de Vaca (4), La Salle(5), and others came along. They used the forest in much the same way that the Karankawas did. Spain and France never colonized the Brazoria County area.

It wasn't until the early 1820's that Stephen F. Austin colonized the area which would become Brazoria County. Then, county forests became commercially exploited.

Chapter 2

Stephen F. Austin to the Civil War

Austin's colonists were the first ones to really exploit the woods. When these pioneers first arrived in the area, the forests were very much in a primeval state. However, the pioneers went about quickly to change all of this. Mostly, they had brought their own tools with them. Therefore many of them didn't make immediate use of the pecan trees to make tool handles and other implements. The first practical use of the woods was in building log cabins, barns, tool sheds and other things of this nature.

Typical methods were the use of axes to fell the trees, saws to cut the logs to the desired length and broad axes to notch and shape the end of the logs. Before long, pit mills, a method off cutting logs into lumber was established. It was at this point that the sawmilling industry really began.

Slave labor was used to establish much of this. One common way was to for one planter to rent skilled slaves to another planter to cut up the wood. To accomplish this, pit mills, especially in the earliest days, were used. A pit mill was one in where a pit was dug, then a platform placed equidistant between the top and bottom and bottom of the pit. Then, a man on top of the platform and one below it would have a long saw in a guide. Draft animals would move the log back and forth across the platform until the boards were made.

An illustration of this method is shown on p.28

However, pit milling was very labor intensive. Better methods soon replaced the pit mills. But, animal power was still used for other timbering purposes. For many operations, this was done until well into the 20th century. (1)

Some early sawmills

The first known sawmill in Texas was in operation at San Augustine In 1819. It was water powered. (2) The first one in Brazoria County was started in 1832 on Chocolate Bayou near present day Alvin. It washed away in the 1832 floods. Stephen Richardson was the operator. After this, he moved to a site near Liverpool. The mill near Liverpool is the only known water powered mill to have operated in the county. A low water dam was built across the bayou. This dam created a millpond with a waterfall to operate the wheel. Much of this milled lumber was sent to Mexico. The mill operated for several years as a saw mill until the timber ran out.

Later it was modified to be a grist mill. It is known that in April 1836 that lumber from his mill was used to fortify Galveston Island.(3) This mill was located on Chocolate Bayou near Liverpool. It was on the W.D.C. Hall property. This mill is mentioned in the probate records of the county, William Harris Estate #233, Feb.5, 1833 as part of the inventory. It is not known precisely how long the mill was in operation, but it was not running during or after the Civil War. (4) Later saw mills in the county were powered by steam until the 20th century.

At least one other non- plantation saw mill was in operation in the 1830's. This comes from an ad placed in THE PEOPLE newspaper in Brazoria on April18, 1838. It states that 10,000 logs were wanted by the Velasco Steam Sawmill Company. The logs were to be of ash, cottonwood, cedar, sycamore, walnut, live oak, and cypress. They also had to be of certain dimensions. Eugene Swan was the agent. It does not state the purpose of such a large order. Also unknown are the dates that this mill ran.

Also, prior to the Civil War, the Dance Family had quite an operation in East Columbia. This operation was running by the late 1840's or the early 1850's. This family is perhaps best known for the pistols they made for the Confederacy. But, before then they had set up a machine shop, cotton presses and a grist mill. The lumber they got to house all this came from a saw mill they had built. The timber was from an area known as the cedar breaks.

Brief descriptions are given on the Plantations known to have had sawmills.

- John Sweeny Plantation - John Sweeny purchased the land in Western Brazoria County in1835. It was known to have had a saw mill on it. (6)
- Isaac Tinsley - He bought his property in 1839 and settled there c.1842. Family tradition states that he got the lumber for his house from the nearby cedar breaks south of present day West Columbia. Then, he milled the lumber himself.(7)
- Peach Lake, later the Van(n) Plantation – was first owned by Judge R.J. Townes It began operating as a plantation in the late 1830's or early 1840's. In 1860Henry Van purchased the place. (8)
- Francis Bingham - Mr. Bingham first settled his on his property in1823. A saw mill was known to be running there by1831. Most of the original property is still in family hands.(9)
- Peach Point – First settled in 1832 by James Perry and Emily Austin Bryan Perry. A saw mill was reported as being there. (10)
- Low Wood - This Plantation was started by Robert and David Mills in the 1840's. The Mills Brothers were also well known bankers and merchants of their time and place Low Wood was the biggest producer of sugar in Texas in the 1850's. Most of the Plantation is now part of the Clemens unit of the Texas department of criminal justice. (11)

These were the only plantations known to operate saw mills that the author could find any information on. Other plantations may have had them. Also, it is unknown when the these plantations got their saw mills running or when the mills stopped running. All of these mills were steam powered and all were on sugar plantations. Sugar production required a lot of fuel whether the sugar mill was steam heated or heated directly by fire. Where did the fuel come from? Let's look at the Jackson Plantations, which may be considered to be typical of plantation operations. Abner Jackson was a major producer of sugar in the county. (12)

In 1862, for example, 132 Hogsheads of sugar and 63 Barrels of molasses were produced. (13) This required 1200 cords of wood. (14) Out of 5628 acres owned, 230 were planted in sugar, 335 in cotton, 335 in corn. (15) So, while much land was producing revenue, quite a bit of the land was being cleared for several reasons. For one thing, the land lost its productivity after a while. (16)Then, new land could be ready to be planted. (17) Also, the wood could age and be readily available as fuel. Then the old land could regrow and the cycle would start over One name that this method of agriculture is known as is "slash and burn."Many of these mills were known to be combined with other plantation functions such as grist mill or a cotton gin.

Several unknowns exist though. For instance it's unknown when the mills began or ceased operating. Also unknown is whether these mills were circular or sash saws. This is not a treatise on plantation history. However, plantation operations are a big part of this story.

Chapter 3

Reconstruction to World War I

Unfortunately, little material exists about the saw mills that were active in this era. Some of the plantations carried on as before, at least for a while. Lake Jackson Plantation is one example. From 1870 until 1900, sugar operations were carried on there. Others, such as Peach Point and the Bingham Plantation, quickly became cattle ranches, but they are still owned by descendants of the original families. Most plantations have long ago been subdivided. Some are now prison farms.

A discussion about saw mills on prison farms will have more detail about these prison farms on later in this chapter.

Some of the plantations carried on by share cropping. After a while, this didn't work out very well. Some typical Strobel comments were something about a place being abandoned or very little of its being worked. As we have seen, no plantation had never been entirely cleared. Also, most of the rest was left to grow back into wilderness. Considering that with the semi - tropical climate of the Upper Coast of Texas, and all of the other factors, there was, and is still, quite a lot of timber still around in Brazoria County.

Some saw milling activity, however, is known to have existed from 1865 to 1900.

One example is on the Lake Jackson Plantation. This however is only inferred. The plantations' original owners had been bought out by 1873. The plantation got its labor by means of the notorious Convict Lease System. Lake Jackson Plantation began leasing convicts about 1873. Ward, Dewey, and Company was the leasing firm. (1) The allusion to the sawmill comes from an 1878 company inventory which states that there were portions of a sawmill, but no saw. (2) This could

6

mean different things. Possibly, the mill was being overhauled. Another possibility is that it was a holdover from when the Jacksons owned the plantation.

Also mentioned in the period from1865 to 1900 is the ownership of a sawmill by Charlie Brown. It will be necessary to give a brief biography of Mr. Brown.

Charlie Brown was an Illiterate ex – slave born in Virginia in the late 1820's. He arrived in Brazoria County in about 1865. (3) He died the richest man in the county, a millionaire, in 1920. He did this through a combination of hard work, persistence, shrewdness, and, no doubt, some luck. He bought some land below West Columbia, known as the cedar breaks. (4) Then he harvested the timber and shipped it by barge down the Brazos River to furniture manufacturers. (5) He had obtained a sawmill before he died in 1920. It is known that he had a close ties to the Dance Brothers. Much of land the he purchased belonged to the Dances.

It isn't known if the mills he bought had first belonged to the Dances. An ad in the Brazoria Independent, in 1881, mentions a sugar plantation for sale. It lists the improvements. Among those improvements is a saw mill. (6)

Sawmills on Prison Farms

Sawmills, as stated earlier, were located on prison farms in Brazoria County for many years. All of these units as they are called today are parts of former plantations. One of them, Clemens seems to never had a saw mill. Ramsey had a saw mill for many years. A brief description and time table will be given.

Clemens – Is 10 miles west of Freeport and 5 Miles east of Brazoria. It's the oldest state run prison farm in the county. Most of the land came from the the biggest part of the old Low Wood plantation. This unit was acquired by the state in 1899. (7)

- Ramsey - Located 10 miles north of Angleton. Now has been subdivided into Ramsey I, Ramsey II, and Ramsey III; It is a composite of the Waverly, Drayton, Quarl, Smith, and Palo Alto Plantations. This unit was acquired by the state in 1908. (8) A saw mill was on it by at least 1924, (9) and a it operated there until about 1970. (10)

7

- Darrington - Was one of the plantations of Major Abner Jackson. (11) This unit was acquired by the State in 1918. (12) It is assumed by the author that a mill was running by 1924. The reason for this assumption is based on the lumber that was sold from it, according to the governor's annual prison report of 1919. (13) It couldn't be determined when this saw-mill ceased operations.
- Retrieve _ another former Jackson Plantation. (14) This unit was also bought by the state in 1918. (15) It couldn't be determined from the annual reports which year that the saw mill on this property was started. The last time it was mentioned as running was by the 1967 TEXAS ALMANAC. (16)

The sugar industry had all but vanished. This was true for the entire old "Sugar Bowl" of Texas. The Brazos River flood of 1899 was a major setback. (17) On top of all of that was the big Galveston hurricane of 1900. (18)

And yet despite these weather phenomena, the area recovered fairly rapidly. Railroads were being built in a big way. (19) Oil in1902 (20) and sulfur in 1910 (21) were discovered. New towns, notably Sweeny in1909 (22) and Freeport in1912 (23) had begun. And, the record of saw milling recommences. Saw mills were in operation near "New "Velasco by 1908, the old town having been destroyed in a hurricane in1875. (24) By 1891, another Velasco had been built four miles upriver from the original town. (25) Its saw mills were advertised in a promotional brochure by the town of Velasco in 1908. (26)

Two sawmills were running in the Anchor area by World War I. In 1917 the first one had been installed by J.M. Frost. (27) Another one in the Anchor area was running by 1919. (28) A Mr. Sparks had put this mill in. Unfortunately, it is not known when either of these mills ceased operating.

One saw mill is known to have existed near present day Clute by c. 1915. It ran until c.1928. The photograph in this book, on p.19 tells the story (29). Another saw mill during the World War I era and beyond was operating in Brazoria; It stood where the Brazoria Lumber Yard stood for many years.

That mill had shut down by c. 1939(30). Also during World War I, there were four plants for making live oak nails.

One such plant was located in Hasima, some four miles west of Sweeny on what was then the St. Louis, Brownsville and Mexico railroad tracks (now, the Union Pacific tracks.) Two of these factories were also located in Brazoria and one in Sweeny(31).

Chapter 4

After World War I

A sawmill was in operation in West Columbia from about 1936 until about1962.

It was located on Hwy 35 west of the intersection of Hwy 36, where the Baytown Seafood restaurant is today (2015). The mill was started in 1936 by C.P. Alexander. He moved from Mississippi to East Texas in the 1930's, and then stayed there for a few years. After that, he started his mill, which was known as C.P. Alexander and Son. This particular mill was powered for at least the last 10 years of its operation by a huge diesel engine. Other machines, such as planers and joiners were powered by electricity. Of course, the electricity was run off the generator from that same motor. The main blade was six feet in diameter.

Mostly the wood to be milled was gotten was from pecan and oak trees. Some cypress wood was cut, too. Most of the wood that was cut went into building such things as board roads and utility mats for access to oil and natural gas fields. Some of the wood went into making bridge timbers. Possibly, some of the wood was made into railroad cross ties. Some of the cypress went into making boats locally. Many of these local boats are still around, able to take whatever the Gulf Coast climate can dish out. C.P. Alexander died in c. 1951, and his son, C.P. Alexander, Jr. took over.

The mill was closed down in 1962 when, according to Pete Alexander, "Pecan quit being popular and was replaced by pine". Of course, there's a very limited quantity of native pine in Brazoria County. (1)

Two sawmills are known to have operated near Liverpool in the 1940's and the1950's. In the early 1940's, Fred Law of Alvin built and operated a(gasoline -?) motor-powered mill on the east side of Chocolate

Bayou north of Hwy. 35 on M.H. Coffeys property. The mill ran for four or five years. It closed down when the timber supply had been exhausted. (2)

Another (gasoline?)- motor-powered mill near Liverpool was running in the early 1950's on the Liverpool Spur road; aka C.R. 192. It was owned and operated by an East Texas firm, and it too, didn't run very long. (3)

While the mills at Liverpool were operating in the eastern part of the county, other mills were starting up in western Brazoria County. Pete Hubbard began his mill north of Hwy. 35 near the Brazoria – Matagorda county line in 1952. He moved his operation in 1955. This later mill was located northwest of the intersection of S.H.35 and F.M.1459 on F.M. 1459. Located about half way between the road intersection and present day Camp Karankawa, This mill had quit running by the late 1950's or early 1960's. (4)

County timber production was still running strong immediately after World War II. THE HANDBOOK OF TEXAS, 1st edition states that Brazoria County ranked 4th in the state in 1947 in timber production. THE TEXAS ALMANAC, from the late 1940's to the early 1950's stated much "much hardwood exported ", while neighboring Matagorda County was described as having some hardwood exported. From then until the mid-1960's Brazoria County was described as having "*some* hardwood exported" while Matagorda County had "*limited* hardwood exported." After that, timber production in the county wasn't mentioned in THE TEXAS ALMANAC. Yet, production continues.

The Johnny Jones Mill

Note: The following comes from interviews with Manuel Stark, Pete Runnels, and Sehon Warneke. According to Mr. Stark, Johnny Jones ran his mill from about 1971 until about 1983. Johnny Jones was the owner and operator of the mill. This mill was located near Churchill, about ½ mile west of the Sportsman Span bridge. Mr. Runnels supplies further information. He states that the mill cut wood with a circular power saw. He also states that the finished product was pallets made of oak wood. Dow Chemical in Freeport was the main customer. Mr. Jones pulled out of his operation when Dow Chemical said that it needed pallets which would better stand up to its chemical products.

Sehon Warneke, a lifelong resident and businessman in the county states that railroad cross ties were also made at this mill.

CANADIAN MILLWORKS

Most of this section of this manuscript is based on interviews, Oct. 2015, with Nancy Stephens of Port Freeport and Nat Hickey of the City of Freeport. The author feels that no history of wood milling in the county is complete without this information.

Ms. Stephens states this. Canadian Millworks is not based in Canada, despite its name. This company was started in Canadian, Texas, by Charles Vignall. The company made mostly door jambs and casings. The big problem was that the wood came from Brazil. So, he decided to cut costs by having wood shipped directly by water. In order to finance this move, 85%of his holdings in Canadian were sold to a Dutch company. Then, he made the move to Freeport. In 1983 land was leased from the port, a building was built, and operations commenced. As was stated above, wood came from Brazil. Types of wood used were Banak, Luann, and Purple Heart. Mostly, it was it was the Banak and Luann that were utilized. Purple heart was used mostly for paneling in the offices. The wood came in extremely rough. So, the wood had to be planed smooth and kiln dried. After that, this lumber could be fabricated into another product. While the plant in Freeport continued making its original product, it soon branched out into other wood products. These largely consisted of rosettes and other decorative items. But that wasn't all that was made. Nothing was wasted. Sawdust was collected by gigantic vacuum pumps, which picked up the dust while wood was being milled.

After that, the dust was stored in large bins on top of the roof. Then, it was bagged and sold. Much of this sawdust was sold to cattle barns in the area, notably in Wharton County. Unfortunately this operation came to a close in Freeport.

In November, 1986, Canadian Millworks ceased its Freeport operations. There may have been several reasons. The opinion of Nancy Stephens, who is mentioned at the beginning of this chapter, is this. Too much attention was paid to the specialty items and not enough to the things they did best like the door jambs and casings. Canadian Millworks relocated to The Woodlands, Texas. In 1989 Port Freeport bought back the lease. After that, the building was upgraded and is now known as Warehouse 51 at the harbor. Canadian Millworks in Freeport is now just a memory. (5)

CECIL STARK MILL later STARK INC.

The lone mill still operating in the late 20th century and early 21st century is Stark Inc., located just east of Danciger, Tx in the western part of Brazoria County. Most of the rest of this part of the manuscript is taken directly from interviews with Manuel Stark and his brother Cecil Stark. Manuel provided 90+%of the information. Much of the technical information of this period comes from the Stark brothers. Also, more information is available due to better documentation and many people still are alive who have first-hand knowledge and still remember many things.

The land where the Stark mill now stands was bought from Glen Denson. The original Stark mill was pieced together from other saw mills from East Texas. Since then, improvements and additions have been made. For example, the original blade was a band saw. This is common in many places throughout the world. It was quickly discovered that with the hard wind twisted wood that predominates in the County, the blade frequently broke, and had to be repaired and/or replaced. So, from then on, a circular saw of 60" diameter has been used.

Other improvements include the use of a conveyor belt to move the saw wood to the blade. Also, none of the wood is wasted. What was discarded in the old days is being ground up to make mulch, or is sent to pulpwood mills in other areas. (6)

Chapter 5

Progress in Safety and Technology

Quite a number of innovations came about after the turn of the 20th century. Railroads, while already in place, caused a number of mills to be built beside them. Animal power, which has been mentioned previously, gave way to mechanized means of getting logs out of the woods. While cutting the harvested timber had already been improved, more were yet to come. Furthermore, the cutting of the timber was made much easier. The wood that came out of these mills was largely destined for a local market. And though local markets are still important, outside markets increased in importance. A more detailed look into these developments will happen as this work progresses.

In the 1830's, when the wood-milling industry in Texas began, OSHA and EPA did not exist. A lot of very dangerous practices went on. The use of personal protective gear was, at best, optional. During the plantation era, an unfortunate slave could be whipped. Also, the means of harvesting the timber had changed little in several centuries. Axes and saws were still the main methods of harvesting wood until well into the 20th Century.

Horses, mules, and oxen were the main ways that the raw timber was hauled out of the woods. Methods of processing timber were often very wasteful. The work was hard and dangerous with little pay. A few examples of this have been shown already. Modern methods, laws, equipment, and innovations have curtailed the danger and drudgery drastically. But make no mistake. Harvesting and processing timber is still rough and dangerous work in which you need to constantly be on your toes.

Animal power ceased to be used about 1920 as the main means of hauling logs out of the woods. After that, winch trucks were the main means of skidding wood for a long time. Also, logs were loaded onto a logging truck with a winch truck. Logging trucks, as they are known now, came out at about this same time. Then, in the1960' came tractors with winches and/or forklift attachments.(7)

Perhaps the greatest improvement in harvesting and gathering wood came about when chain saws became available. The early chain saws, which first came out in Europe in the 1920's, were bulky, heavy, and wheeled, and required two people to run them. Andreas Stihl patented these. By 1941, however, U.S. troops were bringing chain saws home.

One person saws came out by 1945. This was accomplished by means of aluminum alloys. In 1947, Joseph Buford Cox invented the chipper saw chain, the basic design in use now. This was inspired by observing how timber beetle larvae chewed both across and with the wood at the same time. McCulloch Motors debuted the then world's lightest chain saw, 25 pounds, in 1949.

This was the first practical and relatively light chain saw to come on the market. While these innovations in lightness and efficiency were happening, others were, too.

Most of these other changes had to do with safety and being ecologically friendly. In 1964 Stihl introduced the first anti – vibration handle. In 1973 Husqvarna created the automatic chain break. This is a lever that stops the chain after a kick back. By 1980 & 1983, Husqvarna had introduced a chain saw with mostly light weight and / or plastic parts. In 2011 Stihl's MSA 160 C – BQ lithium – ion saw made its appearance. It would run for 35 minutes. By 2011 Stihl's Wood Boss was invented and produced 50 % fewer emissions. (8)

NOTE: This chapter is not a plug or endorsement for any one company, companies, or their products. This part of the manuscript is about the progress in safety and technology. So, it becomes necessary to state injuries and fatalities.

Unfortunately, records are incomplete on this subject. This is especially true of the era prior to the 20th Century. Therefore it's mostly recollections of eyewitnesses and often third-hand information that must be relied on.

In c.1920 a man lost his leg in a timbering accident. One version states that the man was chopping a tree down and that he somehow cut into his leg with an axe. Another version is that a load of logs rolled off a railroad car. He survived, but his legs were crushed.

Sehon Warneke states that in the late 1950's or early 1960's at a mill west of the San Bernard River there was a sawmill fatality. On November 5, 1971, a 54-year-old West Columbia man died whenhis coveralls were caught in a saw blade. (9) Reportedly, his body was cut into four equal pieces.

Unfortunately, these are the only injuries and/or fatalities that the author was able to locate. It's not that he wishes that there were more. It's simply that that the documentation for more doesn't seem to exist.

TYPICAL PIT MILL, EARLY 1800'S, FROM SAWDUST EMPIRE BY ROBERT BAKER

Top: This Sweeny photograph, taken in 1918, shows a team of mules pulling a wagon loaded with logs. Grover Cleveland Redding is riding the mule, while Frank Orr stands on the wagon.

Bottom: Oxen pulling a load of wood down a Sweeny street in 1912.

FOUNDATION FOR STEAM ENGINE FOR GOVERNMENT SAW MILL DURING WW I - BY LAKE BEN (BEND) ON OLD ANGLETON ROAD NEAR CLUTE TX

The saw mill was operated by Mr. Sanford A. Woodruff who owned the land. The mill furnished Oak wood to the government for ship building In WW I. The mill was near the railroad and that made for easy shipping of the lumber. According to family members the mill operated about 10 years. Some of the Woodruff family still live in the Brazosport area today (2008).

Mr. Perry Maxie Brown, father of Dixie Brown & Ford Brown, worked at the mill and in an accident lost his leg. (Information from Hazel West, Robert Woodruff & Ford Brown. -- Photo courtesy of Doris Long Murrell)

Courtesy , Texas Prison Museun, Huntsville, Tx

Ramsey Unit, TDCJ, c. 1935

LOAD OF LOGS FROM THE PRISON BOTTOM TO BE SAWED INTO PRISON LUMBER

RAMSEY SAWMILL IN OPERATION , c.1935, COURTESY OF BRAZORIA COUNTY HISTORICAL MUSEUM AND DAN HESSNER

CANADIAN MILLWORKS LOAD OF RAW LUMBER c.1985, COURTESY OF NANCY STEPHENS, PORT OF FREEPORT

PROCESSING LUMBER CANADIAN MILLWORKS, c. 1985 COURTESY OF NANCY STEPHENS, PORT OF FREEPORT

PROCESSING LUMBER, CANADIAN MILLWORKS, c. 1985, COURTESY OF NANCY STEPHENS, PORT OF FREEPORT

A view looking east, S___ Inc. sawmill, Oct. 2015

Chapter 6

Prospects

Nearly all of the information in this part of the manuscript was provided by Manuel Stark, President of Stark Inc., Danciger, Tx. As has been mentioned previously, Stark Inc. is currently the only mill still running in the county. Mr. Stark states the following.

There is still plenty of marketable timber left in the upper coast of Texas. This is especially true in Brazoria and Matagorda Counties. Unfortunately, not all of this is available. For one thing, the San Bernard Wildlife Refuge has taken almost all of the available land in the immediate vicinity of the company mill. Therefore, no logging can be done there. Also, as of this writing (April, 2016) Brazoria County is in the middle of a building boom. The big trees that must go are being reduced to wood chips. This is ecologically friendly and politically correct. This practice, however, does nothing to help the logging industry.

The Starks are, in fact, almost out of the saw mill business. They have, instead, gone into other ventures in order to stay afloat. These would include, but not be, limited to, such as things land clearing, dirt work of all types, and custom hauling. Some saw milling work is still done, however.

East Texas' piney woods region has always been and always will be the state's primary source of timber. Some saw milling goes on in the post oak belt and hill country of Texas.

So, while logging and wood milling have existed in the county for nearly 200 years, the foreseeable future for that industry in Brazoria

County seems to be rather bleak. And this situation exists, despite the relatively long history of sawmilling in the county, and the great demand for the type of wood that the upper coast of Texas offers still exists.

Chapter 7

Commercially important trees native to Brazoria County

Trees of primary commercial importance

Common name	Scientific name	Primary uses
1. Pecan	*Carya illinoiensis*	Tool handles, furniture, nuts
2. Shumard Oak.	*Quercus shumardi*	Fuel, furniture, cross ties
3. Live Oak	*Quercus virginiana*	Fuel, shipbuilding, cross ties
4. Water Oak	*Quercus nigra*	Similar to Shumard Oak
5. White Ash	*Fraxinus Americana*	log cabins, baseball bats, furniture
6. Loblolly Pine	*Pinus taeda*	Texas' primary lumber tree.
8. Bald Cypress	*Taxodium distichum*	Shipbuilding, boats, shingles
9. Pin Oak	*Quercus palustris*	Similar to Live Oak

Trees of secondary commercial importance

Common name	Scientific name	Primary Uses
1. Sycamore	*Platanus occidentalis*	See the remarks
2. Black Willow	*Salix nigra*	" " "
3. Cottonwood	*Populus deltoids*	" " "
4. Hackberry	*Celtis occidentalis*	" " "
5. Chinese Tallow	*Sapium sebiferum*	" " "

REMARKS ON TREE USES

These other trees are mostly regarded as pest trees or trash trees, of very little to no importance. Mostly they are used in combination with other wood to make construction mats. In the past, this type of wood was laid down and fastened together with individual boards to give access to muddy or otherwise hard to reach places such as for oil or gas drilling. What about Chinese Tallows? A typical rice-farmer or cattle-raiser in Brazoria County has no use for them. A large tallow tree has value to the paper industry. Its wood is soft and white and requires little bleaching. Also while the loblolly pine is listed and has been harvested in the county in the past, it makes up a relatively small percentage of Brazoria County's total forested area.

The table of scientific names for the above species except for the Chinese Tallow tree comes From GUIDE TO SOUTHERN TREES B.Ellwood, S. Harrar, and J. George Harrar, 2nd edition 1962. See p. 40 for the name source of the Chinese Tallow.

Footnotes

Chapter 1
1. A Narrative History of Brazoria County, Texas, 1975, James A. Creighton, 1975, p.444
2. The Karankawa of Texas, 2005, Greg Roza, p.56
3. Roza, pp 13- 27
4. Roza, p.42
5. Roza, pp. 43 & 44

Chapter 2
1. Interview with Michael Bailey
2. SAWDUST EMPIRE AND THE TEXAS LUMBER INDUSTRY 1983, Robert D. Baker, p.2
3. Handbook of Texas Online; subject, Stephen Richardson
4. THE HISTORY OF LIVERPOOL, TEXAS, AND ITS PEOPLE, 1996, J.W. Moore, p.71
5. Creighton, p.244
6. AN OVERVIEW OF THE DEVELOPMENT OF AN HISTORIC LANDSCAPE ON THE SAN BERNARD RIVER AND A HISTORY OF THE LEVI JORDAN PLANTATION, 2004, Martha Doty Freeman, p.62
7. Freeman, p. 59 37
8. Freeman, p.61
9. Freeman, p.63
10. Freeman, p.55
11. TALES FROM THE BRAZOS, 2006, Marie Beth Jones, pp. 139 & 140, excerpted from the GALVESTON NEWS, Nov. 22, 1853
12. Creighton, p.205

13. SUGAR, PLANTERS, SLAVES, AND CINVICTS, 2006, Joan Few. p.12
14. Few, p.172
15. Few, p.12
16. Few, p.172
17. Abigail Curlee, Ph.D. Thesis, p.154

Chapter 3

1. Few, p.97
2. Few p.121
3. Creighton, p.264
4. The Houston Chronicle, by Harvey Rice, 3-11-2015
5. Harvey Rice, 3-11-2015
6. The Independent, Brazoria, Tx ; August 26, 1881
7. Texas Prison Board Annual Report, 1900
8. " " " ", 1909
9. GROING UP ON THE BIG RAMSEY, MEMOIRS OF A PRISON BRAT M.D. Seay, 1983, p.26
10. THE TEXAS ALMANAC lists industries for each prison unit, but did not list the Ramscy sawmill in the 1971-1972 edition.
11. Few, p.35
12. Texas Prison Board Annual Report, 1919
13. Texas Prison Board Annual Report, 1924
14. Few, p.35
15. TEXAS PRISON BOARD ANNUAL REPORT, 1919
16. THE TEXAS ALMANAC lists industries for each prison, but did not list the Retrieve sawmill in the 1968-1969edition.
17. Creighton, p. 282
18. Creighton, p. 292
19. Creighton, p. 321
20. Creighton, p. 324
21. Creighton, p.324
22. Creighton, p.325
23. Creighton, p.324
24. NEW HANDBOOK OF TEXAS, Vol. 6, p.719
25. NEW HANDBOOK OF TEXAS, Vol. 6, p.719
26. An excerpt of this brochure can be found at the Brazoria County Historical Museum in Angleton, Texas.

27. Angleton Times, Nov. 30, 1917
28. Ibid, May 23, 1919
29. From interviews with Gerald Shanks and Dan Kessnner, various times
30. From an interview with Sehon Warneke, c. July, 2015
31. Creighton, p.332

Chapter 4
1. Interview with Pete Alexander, c. August, 2015
2. THE HISTORY OF LIVERPOOL AND ITS PEOPLE, 1996, p. 71, J.W. Moore
3 Moore, p.71
4. Interviews with Manuel Stark and Pete Hubbard, c.July, 2015
5. Port Freeport Annual Report, History of the Port, 1989
6. Interviews with Manuel and Cecil Stark, various times 2008 – 2015
7. POPULAR MECHANICS, Oct.12, 2012, Amanda Green
8. THE BRAZOSPORT FACTS, Nov. 11, 1971

Chapter 6
1. FAMOUS TREES OF TEXAS, Texas Forest Service, December, 1971, p.111

Bibliography

Books
a. A Narrative History of Brazoria County, Texas; James A. Creighton
b. An Overview of the Development of an Historic Landscape on the San Bernard River, Brazoria county, Texas and a History of the Levi Jordan Plantation; Martha Doty freeman.
c. Guide to Southern Trees; Ellwood S. Harrar & J. George Harrar, 1962
d. Sawdust Empire & The Texas Lumber Industry; Robert D. Baker
e. Sugar, Planters, Slaves, and Convicts; Joan Few
f. The Handbook of Texas
g. The History of Liverpool, Texas and its People; J.W. Moore
h. The Karankawa of Texas, Greg Roza
i. The Texas Almanac, 1968-1969 and 1970-1971 editions
j. The New Handbook of Texas

Interviews
a. Pete Alexander
b. Michael Bailey, Curator of the Brazoria County Historical Museum
c. Dan Kessner
d. Nat Hickey
e. Pete Hubbard
f. Webb Jones
g. Pete Runnels
h. Gerald Shanks

    i.   Manuel and Cecil Stark

    j.   Nancy Stephens

Newspaper Articles

    a.   The Angleton Times

    b.   The Brazosport Facts

    c.   The independent, Brazoria

    d.   The People Newspaper, Brazoria

    e.   The Houston Chronicle

Various Publications

    a.   Abigail Curlee, Ph.D thesis, University of Texas, 1932

    b.   City of Velasco brochure, 1908

    c.   Growing up on the Big Ramsey, M.D. Seay, 1983

    d.   Port of Freeport, Annual Report, 1989

    e.   Texas Prison Board Annual Report; various years, various authors

# on map	Name on map	location on map page #	Text p.#	Operation dates
1	William Harris Estate	40	3	c.1820's - c.1840's
2	Velasco Steam Saw Mill	40	3	1837 - ?
3	John Sweeny Plantation	39	4	c.1830's - ?
4	Isaac Tinsley Plantation	40	4	c.1830's - ?
5	Peach Lake Plantation	39	4	c.1830's - ?
6	Bingham Plantation	39	4	c.1831 - ?
7	Peach Point Plantation	39	4	c.1840's - ?
8	Low Wood Plantation	39	4	c.1840's - ?
9	Lake Jackson Plantation	40	4, 6, 7	Mentioned in 1873
10	Plantation, name unknown	40	7	Mentioned in 1881
11	Dance Brothers, Charlie Brown	39	7	c.1850's - c 1920's
12	Ramsey Unit,TDJC	40	7	1924 - 1970
13	Darrington Unit, TDCJ	39	7	1924 - ?
14	Retrieve Unit,TDCJ	40	8	? - 1966
15	J.M. Frost Mill	40	8	1917 - ?
16	Sparks Mill	40	8	1919 - ?
17	WWI Govenment Mill	40	8	c.1915 - c.1928
18	Name Unknown	39	8	c.1915 - c.1939

19	Plant for making live oak nails	39	8, 9	c.1917 - c.1919
20	Plant for making live oak nails	39	8, 9	c.1917 - c.1919
21	Plant for making live oak nails	39	8, 9	c.1917 - c.1919
22	Plant for making live oak nails	39	8, 9	c.1917 - c.1919
23	Alexander Mill	39	10	c.1936 - c.1962
24	Fred Law Mill	40	10	c.1940 - c.1945
25	Name Unknown	40	11	c.1952 - c.1954
26	1st Pete Hubbard Mill	39	11	c.1952 - c.1954
27	2nd Pete Hubbard Mill	39	11	c.1955 - c.1960
28	Johnny Jones Mill	39	11	c.1971 - c.1973
29	Stark Inc	39	12	1972 - present (2015)
30	Glen Denson Mill	39	12	Running in 1971
31	Canadian Millworks	40	12	1983 -1986

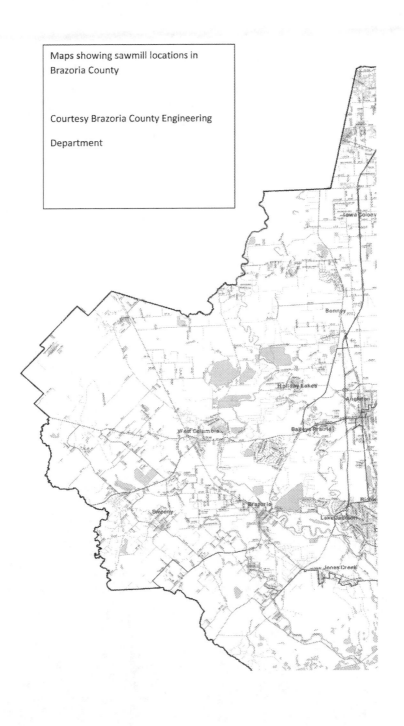

Maps showing sawmill locations in
Brazoria County

Courtesy Brazoria County Engineering

Department

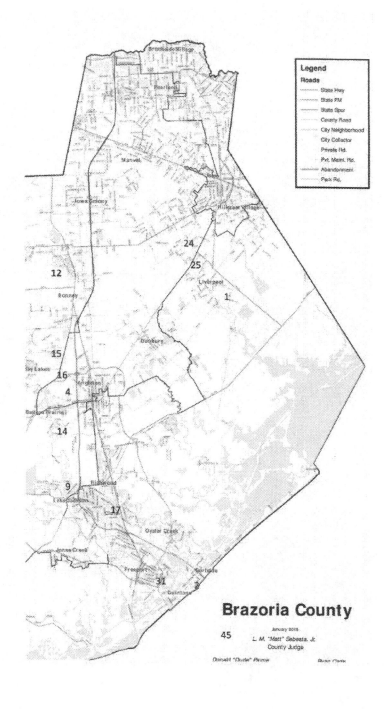

Brazoria County

January 2015

45

L. M. "Matt" Sebesta, Jr.
County Judge

Donald "Dude" Payne   Ryan Cade

Printed in the United States
By Bookmasters